MW01482025

About *Still Ripples*:

This booklet looks at the emotional ripples that can only be expressed through poetic words and phrases. Nothing is still, and life can be exciting when changes happen. A person never knows where exactly they will end up with life's meandering currents, and this 50-page booklet is no exception. Written for all ages, poetry touches the soul, and can be very healing, as well. Viva la poetry!

RHAMONA
Have a great
read!!

Karen He

Other books written by Karen Hein:

Inspired Musings

Bits, Snippets, & Other Works

Karen's Website: www.karenheinpoetry.ca

First Edition

STILL RIPPLES

POETRY BY:
KAREN HEIN

Acknowledgments:

Thanks to the helpful staff at The New View Society, who made my books possible, and also made *The Poetry Show with Karen and Friends* possible.
Thanks to my teachers over the years, who taught me writing tricks and helped me to develop my own style.
Thanks to my family, who supported me, even though they did not always understand my passion for poetry.
Thanks to my friends including (but not limited to): Pat K., Michelle O., Penny H., Angelica B., Yvonne R., Anita T., Allan M., and Sandra O. They put up with every new poem that I had to share over the years.
Thanks to my creative writing group friends: Tea & Ink, Poco Heritage Group, My College Group. They encouraged me and helped me to focus on my professional writing career.
Thanks to Katherine, my worker, who believed in me.
And thanks to my friends at Calendar Club, the Evergreen Cultural Centre, and Parkwood Manor. They have been kind and encouraging.

Note from the Poet:

The booklet, "Still Ripples", is far from being still as the thoughts are turbulent underneath the water's calm ripples. The world is a crazy place sometimes and we need to see what effects our actions make. Skipping rocks creates ripples which touch other aspects of life. For every action there is an equal and opposite reaction. The lake seems so placid until something touches the surface and disturbs the tranquility. But even after it is disturbed, the water becomes calm again and life gets back to normal. So goes the Year, as the planets align to make things happen and the ripple extends to the undercurrents of the whole Universe. For life to continue there must be ripples that change the expected outcome. If everything stayed the same, life would become stagnant and mosquitoes would thrive in the still waters. So, no matter what happens, keep an eye on the origin of the ripple's center. It will keep you focused and able to face the future.

I hope you enjoy this rocky, but hopeful bunch of poems. It always brings me pleasure to share my thoughts with you. Until next time... Enjoy!

Karen Hein

One Little Drop Begins It...

The time has come again
To pray that it will rain.
Showers from the sky
Will wet all the dry.
And little water streams
Will fill all our dreams,
As raindrops gently fall
And send out a call,
For all rivers to meld
And be upheld,
In an awesome display
That will last all the day,
Of waterfall sprinkles
And little roaring tinkles
And rainbow mists of light,
That are ever so bright,
With colors that please
The eyes and tease
The lenses
Of all our senses:
One little raindrop speaks.

Sunset's Gift

Arm in arm
We watch
The glorious sunset
Shine with an orange glow
Down onto the greeny-blue
Ocean waves which
Sparkle with
Little points of
Reflected lights
Back to the
Sandy beach.
Others join us
To admire
Nature's artwork
On this temperate
And
Marvelous
Evening
That holds
The beginning of
A budding
Romance
In its memory.

Create-ality

Create-ality.
The beauty of
Creating
Your own
Reality.
Hopes, wishes, dreams,
That make you happy.
Changes happen
And shake things up a bit.
Got to go
With the flow
And adapt
To the situation.
Love, life, and laughter
Make a
Happy existence,
And
Everyone deserves
To be happy.
So I say,
Dare to see
The future
The way you want it.
It may not be exactly
What you envision,
But it will
Be right
For your needs.
Blend with
The universe
And time will be
Your ally.
Namaste.

Dark Glasses

She sees with sunglasses
All that passes,
And the sun in the sky
Cannot burn her eye:
The UV protection
Prevents that action.
What secret does she keep
As her eyes peep
From the shadow's tint
And the dark glint
That makes her eyes hard to see
Or is it just me?

Eerie Energy

The phone is silent.
No ringing tonite.
All the world
Is at rest.
Hallowe'en calls forth
Strange energy.
It's the end of a season
And the beginning
Of the soul's journey
Through the turning of
The Wheel of the year.
Autumn's leaves
Fall silently
As the world preps
For the coming Winter.
Ghosts of days gone by
Remind us of
The way life was
Before the season
Started to change.
The Harvest Moon
Glows an orange hue
Against a clouded,
Crisp nite sky.
And
Pumpkins smile
Their toothy grins
Against the
Darkness of the
Coming nite.

Winter's Touch

The Snowflake floats and
Lands on my nose.
A little bit of icy cold
That is Winter's touch.
There is a sparkle
In the air
That is the miracle
Of true love's
First admission.
The twinkle in the eye
Speaks of imagination.
Realms of thought
Which have every freedom
And yet are restricted
By Ego's cold logic.
Yet the hope
Of all eternity
Turns the wheel of the year
To cycle anew
As Spring arrives
And Winter's hold
Is loosened from
The Land.

Dismantling Xmas

I eye
The baubles,
Cards,
And tree
Left over
From
A wonderful Xmas
And realize
I have to
Take them down.

Slowly,
With a thought
For each thing,
I remove
The trinkets
And store them
Away
Reluctantly
So they will
Cheer me again
Next year.

Entranced Moment

In a trance,
The kittens watch
The butterflies dance.

The wind blows
The swaying daisies
To and fro.

The gentle breeze
Makes the kittens'
Noses sneeze.

A pool's reflection
Of double vision
Seems to beckon,

And the kittens
Timidly
Raise their mittens

And paw the empty air
Even tho there really was
Nothing there.

Train's Passage

The long
Resounding
Whistle
Of the little
Freight train,
Pierced
The cold,
Mountain air,
As a startled
Flock of crows
Rose off the track,
Into the blue sky
With a great
Flutter
Of feathered
Black wings.
And,
A pair of deer,
Showing their
White tails,
Bounded off
Into
The nearby
Clump
Of green trees.

Covid's Year

Having a hug
Is very snug
But Covid's year
Has made me fear
Of ever feeling close again.
However,
An occasional call
Could heal the stall
Of wounded hearts
Now that we're apart.
And a furry friend
Would see the end
Of lonely days
That won't stay
As people again connect,
It's a sure bet
That the illness spreads
On little threads
Of contact and breath:
It could mean death!
So stay smart
And keep apart
And let us heal the world.

In the Name of Progress

The trees and shrubs
Grown wild for the birds,
Are knocked to the ground,
Because of man's quest for homes.
Everything that once
Was a pleasant nesting ground
Has been destroyed
By the concept of progress.
Nothing is safe
From change,
Because change happens
Untutored and unkind.
Looking with sadness
On the devastation
That was once peaceful,
Brings sadness to my heart,
As wildlife gets displaced
All for the benefit
Of plentiful people.
They don't fathom
The change of scenery
As they happily
Move into condos,
Cold hard buildings
That have no heart.
But,
Nature waits.
Eager to once again
Claim back its territory
As Man moves on
To other things.
War between
Man and Nature
Continues,
For the rest of time:
Nature's resilience
The hope for the future.

Desert Afternoon

The Sun's golden orb:
Sweltering, Burning, Evaporating,
Shines relentlessly
On the prickly, green
Cactus groves
That keep little creatures cool
Under the heatwave's heat.
The air shimmers
As mirages
Of palm-treed oasis
Come and go,
And the thirst
For life-giving water
Keeps a lonely,
Sweat-sweltered
Traveller
Crawling across the sands
Of the desert's unwelcoming
Stretch of sand dunes,
And a circling pair
Of hungry vultures
Mark the traveller's progress
Hoping for
An easy afternoon snack.

Just Crazy!

Crazy!
Mad! Simply Mad!
A little scattered?
These are my labels,
I wear them with pride
As I think strange thoughts
And believe
In far-out things.
Spirit talks synchronicities.
And brings them to my notice.
And the little noises
I hear in my head
I drown out with
The music,
Which become my reality.
Coping with peculiarities
Keeps me writing
To sort it all out.
Sharing my madness
Turns you away.
It is too strange
And very odd,
Not regular at all!
A weirdo for sure!
Nope just crazy, that's all.

Ocean's Fury

The ocean waves sparkle and shimmer
As the sun's rays glimmer.
The peace as the ocean sleeps,
Allows the shadows to creep,
And the night turns the sky
Into riveting clouds that try,
To turn a day's delight
Into another sight
Of blowing wind and gale.
It turns the sail
Into a fight for life
That goes well into the night,
Right to the morn,
Just like a woman's scorn.
And with suddenness of motion,
Calm once more overtakes the ocean,
And seagulls fly again.

Stormy Thoughts

The thoughts
In my mind
Synchronize and twist
In a hurricane
Of anxious wonderings,
As I sift
Oceans of emotions.
Like a little rowboat
Being tossed by
Mighty waves,
I try to syphon
Myself
Into a whirlpool
Of sweet memories
That remind me
Of your smile,
So kind.
When life surges
Back and forth
Like the waves at the beach,
I remember
Standing
Side by side.
Strong in
Our devotion
To life's adventures.

The Blinking Beacon

The crashing waves
Smash with crushing force
The rough, craggy rocks
Upon which
The lonely, chalk white lighthouse sits,
Blinking its flashing silvery light,
Out into the foggy, black nite.
Its signal warns the passing ships
Of the ominous danger
Of straying too close
To the rocky hallows
Of its island.
It sits
In the middle
Of deep water stretching
Between the mainland harbours,
And the peppered islands
That are sprinkled across the ocean's
Vast waters,
Its light, a safe beacon against the darkness.

Open Air Poetry

Outside we sit,
Under the clouds
Reading poetry.
It is like
The sky is listening
And reacting
To the sound of the voice
As it filters
Dappled sounds
Through the trees.
A small audience has gathered
As poetic bliss
Is vocalized
And emphasized
To the birds and the sky.
A pregnant silence
Afterwards,
Seems like
The Gods are
Listening
And assessing
The performance's reflection
Of life's spoken
Eloquence,
Which is poetry's gift.

Pick Your Drink

Coffee - a brilliant
Invention.
Wake up! Socialize!
Choose cream or milk.
Sugar or sweetener swallows
The bitter taste.
Chewy grounds,
Muddy water,
Liquid heat.
Pop a breath mint
To devour
Bad breath.

Tea – straight from
The orient.
Easy on the stomach.
Calming to the mind.
A great watery flavor
Hot or cold.
It can fix your troubles
With its mild
Caffeinated mix.

Juice – squeezed from
Tasty fruits.
Gives energy
With vitamin C
And
Liquid sunshine.
Your go-go
To get moving
On those
Sluggish mornings.
Gets the blood
Moving and
The muscles pumped.

Water – the basis of life.
Clear and cool.
Refreshing and revitalizing.
Liquid, solid, and gas.
The foundation
And origin
Of all creatures.
Purging and cleansing
And necessary for
All of Life's thirsty
Situations.

Real Meal Satisfaction

When I go out to eat
It really can't be beat
To get what you think
Is a really cool drink.
It goes with your meal
On the side, where its real,
Take a few sips
From your parched lips
And wash the food down
And then look around:
All the tables are full.
The food has quite a pull.
It contributes to the finest hour,
That is dining power!

In Step With my Shoes

Trusty runners
Fit my feet
And step with me
As I walk
Thru life.
The soles are worn
But they still have grip
And don't slip
Even when the weather's wet.
The shoes wrap my feet
In comfort and
Tiny grits and gravels
Cannot get to my toes
Because
My shoe coverings
Protect me from
Those little irritants.
My shoes lead the way
And the path I walk
Will be straight and forward
And evenly paced
With each step I take,
Thanks to my shoes.

Magic of Leaves

Maybe the magic of belief
Starts with a tree's leaf.
Every fall without fail
The leaves start to bail.
After another year,
The eye starts to tear
At the loss
And the toss
Of crunchy remains.
But, even children can't refrain
From the fun
As they run
And jump
With a thump
Into the pile
With a smile.
Yet, even so time ticks
And the trees, oh so thick,
Fall asleep
In the deep
Of winter's grip.
As the leaves again slip
Into Spring's
Lifelong thing
Of sprouting again,
A real, true friend.

Love's Senses

If love were a flavor
It would be of
Cinnamon and sugar cookies
And a glass of hot cocoa,
So comforting
To the soul.

If love were a scent
It would be of
Peppermint gum
Being chewed,
So refreshing
To the spirit.

If love were a sight
It would be of
Butterflies
Fluttering through
The air,
So uplifting
To the mind.

If love were a touch
It would be of
The slippery satin robe
That covers me,
So sensuous
To the senses.

If love were a sound
It would be of
The chirp of the robin,
So hopeful
For a morning of new beginnings.

Raindew on Red Rose Petals

Raindew on red rose petals
Glistens like shiny metals,
As it reflects silver dew
On quite a few
Of the flower's
Colorful powers
Of sight and smell
That makes you feel well.
Compared to the light
It's a beautiful sight,
But be careful of the thorns,
Don't view them with scorn.
They will pierce your skin
Because skin is thin.
But, no harm done
Its all in good fun
As we give roses with love
From the hand of a glove.

Wait No More

On the bench
Sits a lonely lady skeleton
Waiting for
The perfect skeleton man
To arrive to make
Her life complete.
She waits an eternity
Because the perfect man
Doesn't exist.
He is a ghost with no
Substance.
A figment
Of her imagination.
She needs to learn
How to complete
Her own life
With her own efforts.
Carve her own pumpkins.
Nobody
Can do it
For her.
Maybe she'll realize
What a folly it is
To wait
On the bench,
And feed the pigeons.

Waiting for Time

Waiting…
For time to tick,
As the moments
Slip from one
To another.
Activity
Makes the minutes
Go by quicker.
Silence is a meditation
Of prayers
And fond thoughts,
That dwindle
As sleep approaches
With the evening hours.
The sun starts
To go West,
And the moon
Appears in the East
As
The clock winds
Forward
To another
Dawn's day,
And the world awakes
And time ticks on
Again.

The Fly's Dilemma

There was a fly
On my windowsill.
I felt sorry for it
And contemplated
Freeing it
From its prison.
The fly flew
Up to the corner
And buzzed the pane.
I took a coffee can,
Caught it,
And
Freed it outside again.
I wonder
Where that little fly
Went to?
It had only
Brief 15 days
To experience life.
I gave it
Another few days
And saved it
From stale existence
Of being trapped
In the house
With me.

Remember the Sun?

The crack in the wall
Shows plaster peeling.
The stained doily covers
The worn top of the table,
That should be an antique,
But instead,
Has been loved
With thoughtless scorn,
Through many year's
Of careless hands.
In the center of the table
Rests a faded old vase
With flowers
That have seen better days.
Passing pit-pattered footsteps
Show on the threadbare hallway rug.
The clock on the mantlepiece
Has stopped,
Exhausted,
And wants new batteries
To work again.
The yellowed windowframe
Highlights
The crying rain
As it drips
Down the dirty glass pane.
A dreary Autumn Day.

People Come and People Go

People come
And people go,
Who am I,
To cause us woe.

We sit there
In our little cares
And wonder why
Everyone stares.

Should we try to smile
And forget our troubles,
To come to peace
In our respective bubbles?

But to share with others
Is not the thing
We keep it smothered,
It sure can sting.

Love's Next step

What once was love
Is now forgone
They've gone and left me,
Now I'm alone.

Their place remains
An empty space
That causes pains
And changes my pace.

As I stumble
With the next phase
I try not to bumble
And make mistakes,

But life's a wonder
And can go asunder
When trying to make
Everything great.

I wish for guidance
Now that I'm free,
To finish the dance,
Its up to me.

Patching Things Up

I'll try to make it better
By sending you a letter.
The thoughts in my mind
Are very, very kind.
And I need you to see
That's the only way to be,
Because life is too small
We should give it our all.
The clock ticks on the wall
And the minutes fall
One by one.
To see the heat of the sun
From the smile on your face
Is your rightful place,
And warms my heart,
Although we are apart.
I will try my best
To try and guess,
The reason that your leaving
Is a fact.
Don't stay away
I pray,
I honor your path
And would rather laugh,
Then see you upset with me.

Heartfelt Remorse

Sorry is a word
That is too often heard.
It should be spoken from the heart:
Apology is an art.
Sincerely spoken
It can fix the broken
And mend the fences
As it breaks down defences.
Let us be forgiven
For being so driven.
Mistakes can happen
So let's keep on laughing.
Things are not as bad
As they are simply mad
And they sometimes seem
To be a bad dream.
Forgotten is best,
Let's give it a rest
And continue without a scene.

Possibilities Abound

Celebrate the world
As it changes everyday,
In every conceivable way.
From the caves
Of old ages,
To the cel phones
And road cones
Of progress.
None-the-less,
Human-kind
Says fine,
And keeps exploring
New stories
Of new lands
Where Man's feet
Have not stepped,
Yet:
Outer space calls.
Landing on Mars
And out to the stars,
People will go
And Mankind will flow
To the next cycle
And cut the umbilical
Of the Motherhood
Of life on Earth.

The Rhythm of the Stars

The stars shine brightly,
And sparkle nightly,
And the town underneath sleeps
In a scene of such peace.
The moon is crossing the sky
And is all but passing by
As the sun's first rays
Bring about a new day.
And rooster's crow
From down below,
As life stirs from sleep
It's time again to keep
The cows milked
And the horses brushed and silked.
The regular routine
Seems quite mundane.
Again, the sun slowly crosses the sky
The day turns to night
And the town sleeps again
Under the stars, where we began.

Colors of Life

These are the colors:
Green as the growing grass,
Blue as the sky above,
Red as the rose's blush,
Pink as the sun's first light at dawn,
Yellow as the buttercup's brass,
Orange as the fruity splash,
Purple as the orchid's bloom,
Rusty as the camouflaged coat,
Black as technology's image,
White as your smile's touch:
These are the colors that make my world go round.

The Checkered Challenge

Black and White
The Chess pieces fight.
Across the checkered board
Slowly they forge.
Each piece is moved
After a good brood,
And thinking ahead,
Forward they are led.
To protect the King
Is the primary thing,
And at the same time
The battle draws lines.
Two hours or more
They fight for the board.
At last,
Time has passed,
And both players wait,
For the other's fatal mistake
That will win them the checkmate,
And leave a barren board behind.

Time to Rhyme

Gotta a Dime?
Get in line
And I'll find the time
To make a rhyme,
That'd be fine
And it'll be a sign,
To get a spine
And redefine
This heart of mine
With a glass of wine.

The Whispering Wind

The Whispering Wind has
A sense of
Elusiveness
As its invisible presence
Flurries
Leaves and papers
In little tornados.
The breath of air
So essential
For life,
Creates
Notes of
Sound
As it
Brushes through
Branches of trees
And man's
Random
Wind chimes.
Sometimes
The breeze
Carries
Whiffs of
Spirits,
Which could be
The angels
Watching
Silently
Over us,
That seem to
Want to speak
To us,
But their voices
Are taken
By the Wind's
Meandering
Way.

Book in a Nook

Sitting in a little nook,
Reading my favorite book,
And as the pages turn
I am fascinated and learn,
About legends and lore,
They are never a bore.
The pages are crispy
And as I look and see
The letters written there
And I can't help but stare
At the illustrations
And pictures they've done.
I admire
The fire
In the story
That they've told,
Which I can't help but compare
To another world, but where?

The End of the Road

At the end of the road
There sat a toad.
He was bumpy and brown,
And he had quite a frown.
He looked at me.
What did he see?
I'll never know,
Because it started to snow,
And the frowning toad
Quickly hopped off the road,
Never to be seen again.

Also available:
Karen Hein's first poetry book,
"Inspired Musings".

(Also on audiobook.)
Available at:
karenh61@hotmail.com
If you like simple, easy to
understand poetry, you will
like this 40-page booklet.
The subjects range from
 fantasy to nature, and
always evoke a response
from the reader. Metaphors
fill the pages and very little
 rhymes. It is original and
 reads like a smooth ice
cream sandwich.

Praise for "Inspired Musings"
 from readers:

"Karen's words weave
wonderfully vivid scenes to
wander through your mind
always returning with a feeling
of calm and appreciation for
the magic around us
everyday."
– Wes K.

"Thoughtful words taking my
mind to far away places.
Making me remember better
days." – Deanna V.

"Met the author, Karen Hein,
this evening for a
book signing and Poetry
reading. She is a very talented
and creative writer. This book
is a gem, not only for yourself
or as a lovely and thoughtful
gift. Her written words create
powerful images and emotions
within. Amazing book!" –
Connie B.

Still Ripples

Also available from Karen Hein:
"Bits, Snippets, & Other Works"
- the book and audiobook.

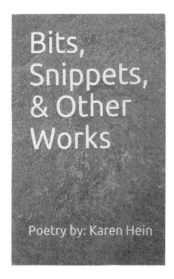

About "Bits, Snippets, and Other works":
This fifty-page booklet from poet, Karen Hein, takes the reader on a romp through the teenage mind, as she questions and learns lessons from her high school adventures earlier in life. This booklet is suitable for all ages. The poetry and small stories take the reader back in time to connect with a younger self. Enjoy the read and feel free to share with friends and family. Watch for more poetic material to come. Viva La Poetry!!

Praise from readers for "Bits, Snippets, & Other Works":

"Every poem brings me back to nature (which I love) and captures the moments in time with great power in every word. The book was very intriguing and touching."
– Theresa F.

"Funny, silly, and heartwarming all condensed into one book. The book brought laughter and moments of serious emotion as well."
– Shirley H.

"Karen's poetry paints a beautifully descriptive picture that makes the writing come to life. The words captivate and illuminate the senses making every page entertaining." – Krystina H.

"Nice mix of short, medium and long poems. A wonderful variety. A pleasant romp through poetic pages. I am looking forward to reading the next book, too!"
– Elizabeth L.

To get your copy, contact:
karenh61@hotmail.com

Still Ripples

Made in the USA
Middletown, DE
06 August 2021